CONTENTS

ISBN 978-1-4234-6552-2

7777 W. BLUEMOUND RD. P.O. BOX 13819 MILWAUKEE, WI 53213

Visit Hal Leonard Online at
www.halleonard.com

Don't Rain on My Parade

from FUNNY GIRL
Words by Bob Merrill
Music by Jule Styne

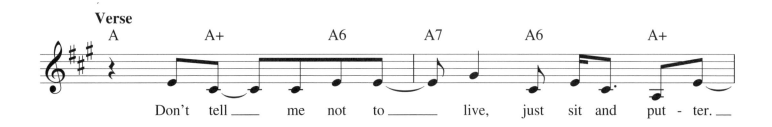

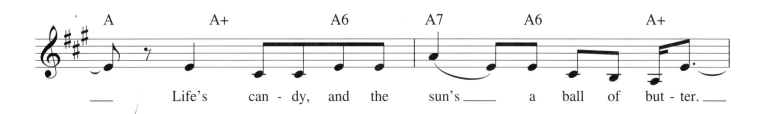

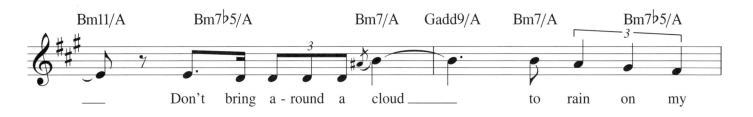

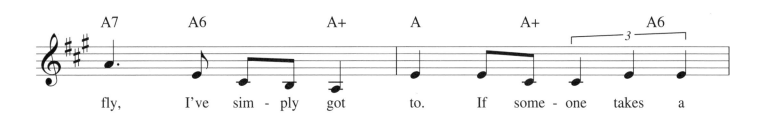

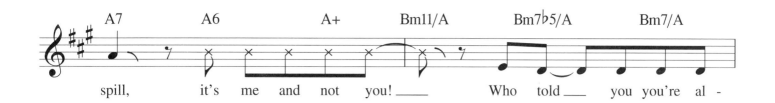

spill, it's me and not you! ___ Who told ___ you you're al -

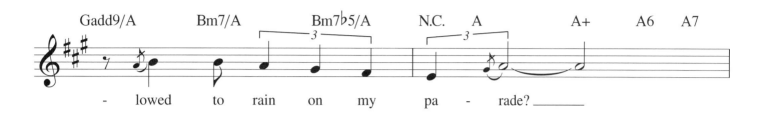

- lowed to rain on my pa - rade? _____

Bridge

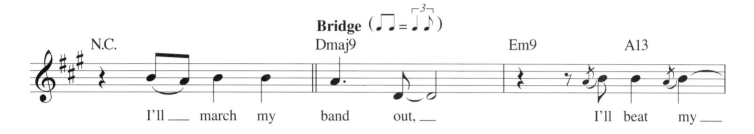

I'll ___ march my band out, ___ I'll beat my ___

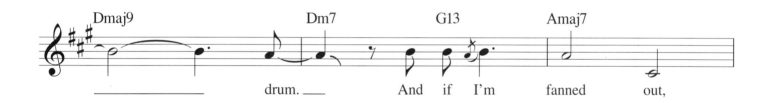

_____ drum. ___ And if I'm fanned out,

your turn at bat, sir, at

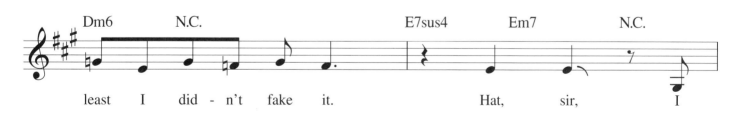

least I did - n't fake it. Hat, sir, I

Verse

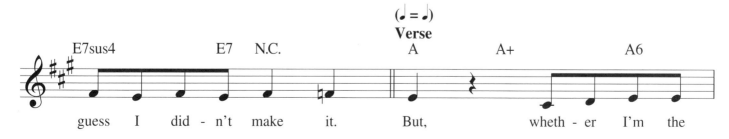

guess I did - n't make it. But, wheth - er I'm the

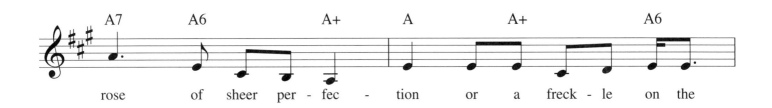

rose of sheer per - fec - tion or a freck - le on the

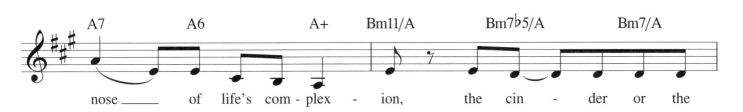

nose _____ of life's com - plex - ion, the cin - der or the

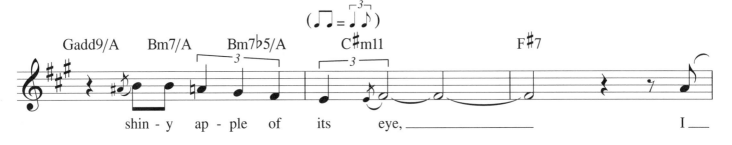

shin - y ap - ple of its eye, _____ I _____

_____ got - ta fly once, I _____ got - ta try once.

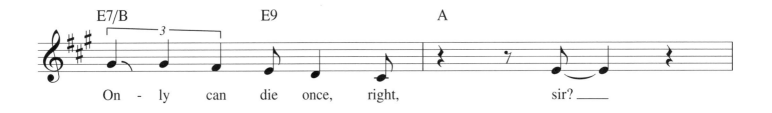

On - ly can die once, right, sir? _____

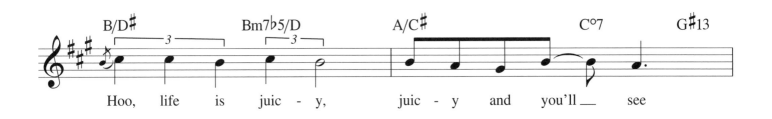

Hoo, life is juic - y, juic - y and you'll _____ see

I got - ta have my bite, sir.

Verse

Get read-y for me,____ love, 'cause I'm a com -

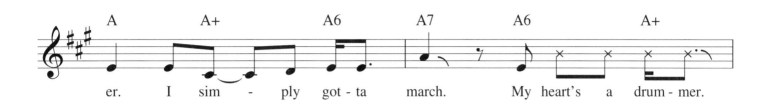

er. I sim - ply got - ta march. My heart's a drum - mer.

Don't bring a - round a cloud ____ to rain on

Gradually faster
Interlude

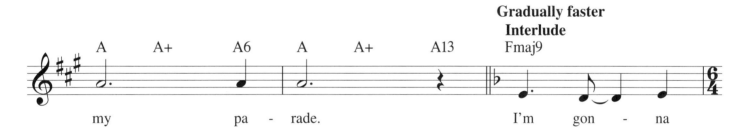

my pa - rade. I'm gon - na

live, and live now. Get what ___ I

want, I know how. One roll ___ for

the whole she - bang, one roll, ___ that

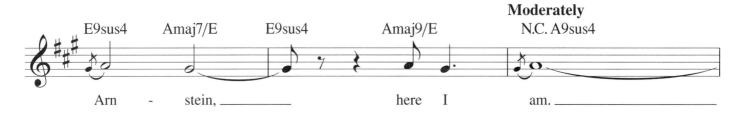

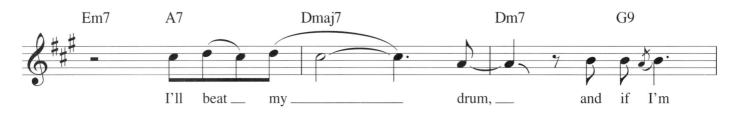

My Man

Words and Music by James Hanley and Gene Buck

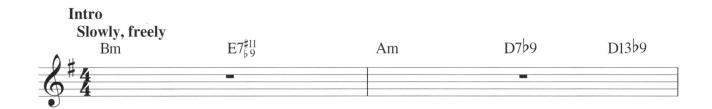

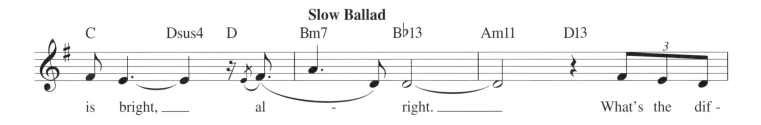

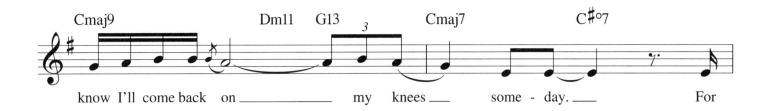

know I'll come back on _____ my knees _____ some - day. _____ For

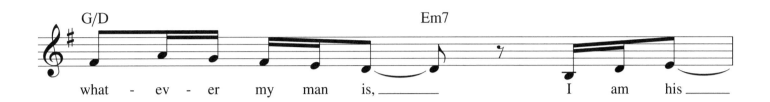

what - ev - er my man is, _____ I am his _____

_____ for - ev - er - more.

Bridge
Brightly, freely

It cost _____ me a lot, but there's one thing that I got, it's

my man. _____ Cold and wet, tired, _ you bet,

but all that I'll soon for - get _____ with my man. _____

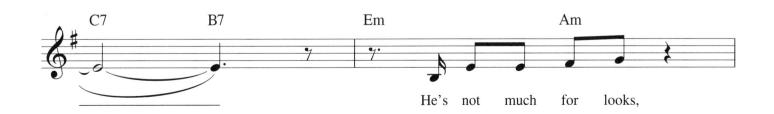

_____ He's not much for looks,

ain't no he-ro out of books, he's my _____ man. ____

____ Two or three girls has he that he likes as

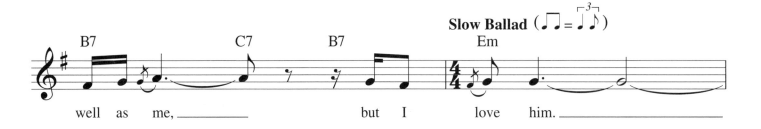

Slow Ballad (♩♩ = ♩ ♪)

well as me, _____ but I love him. _____

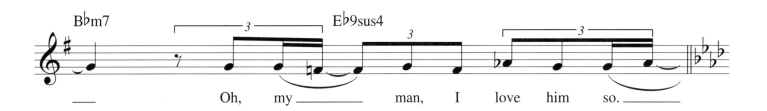

____ Oh, my _____ man, I love him so. _____

Chorus

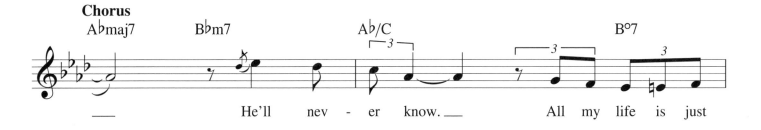

____ He'll nev - er know. ___ All my life is just

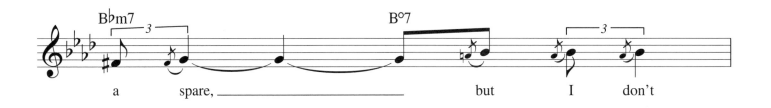

a spare, _____ but I don't

care. When he takes me in his

10

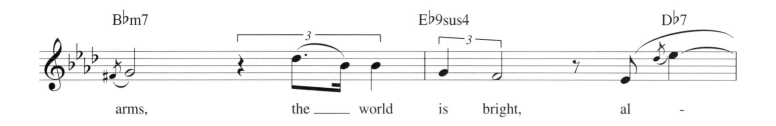

arms,   the ___ world is bright, al -

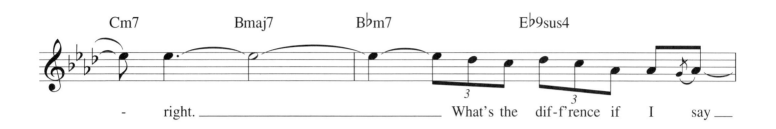

- right. _____ What's the dif-f'rence if I say ___

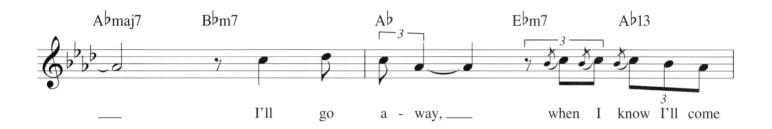

___ I'll go a - way, ___ when I know I'll come

back on _____ my knees _____

some - day.   For what-ev - er my man is,   I am

Slower

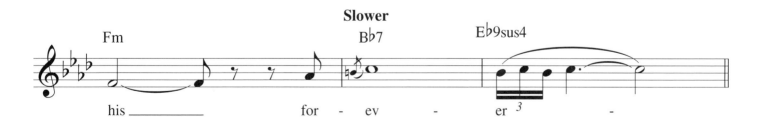

his ___ for - ev - er ___

Outro

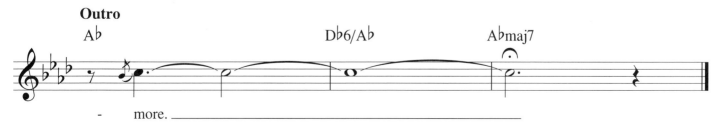

- more. _____

One

from A CHORUS LINE

Music by Marvin Hamlisch
Lyric by Edward Kleban

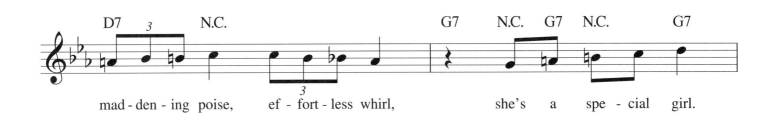

mad - den - ing poise, ef - fort - less whirl, she's a spe - cial girl.

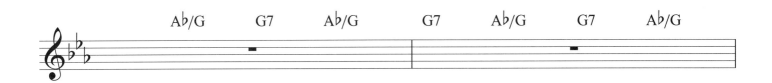

Men: Stroll - ing, can't help

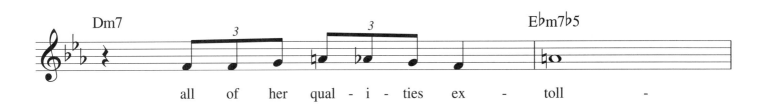

all of her qual - i - ties ex - toll -

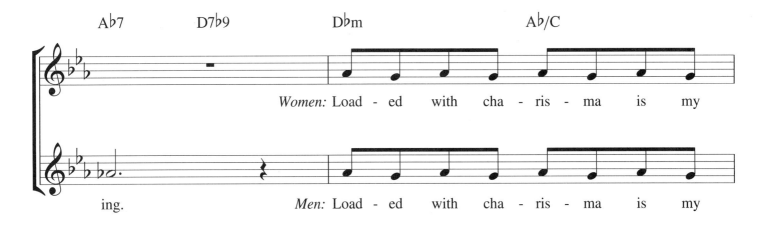

Women: Load - ed with cha - ris - ma is my

ing. *Men:* Load - ed with cha - ris - ma is my

jaun - ti - ly saun - ter - ing, am - bl - ing, sham - bl - er.

jaun - ti - ly saun - ter - ing, am - bl - ing sham - bl - er.

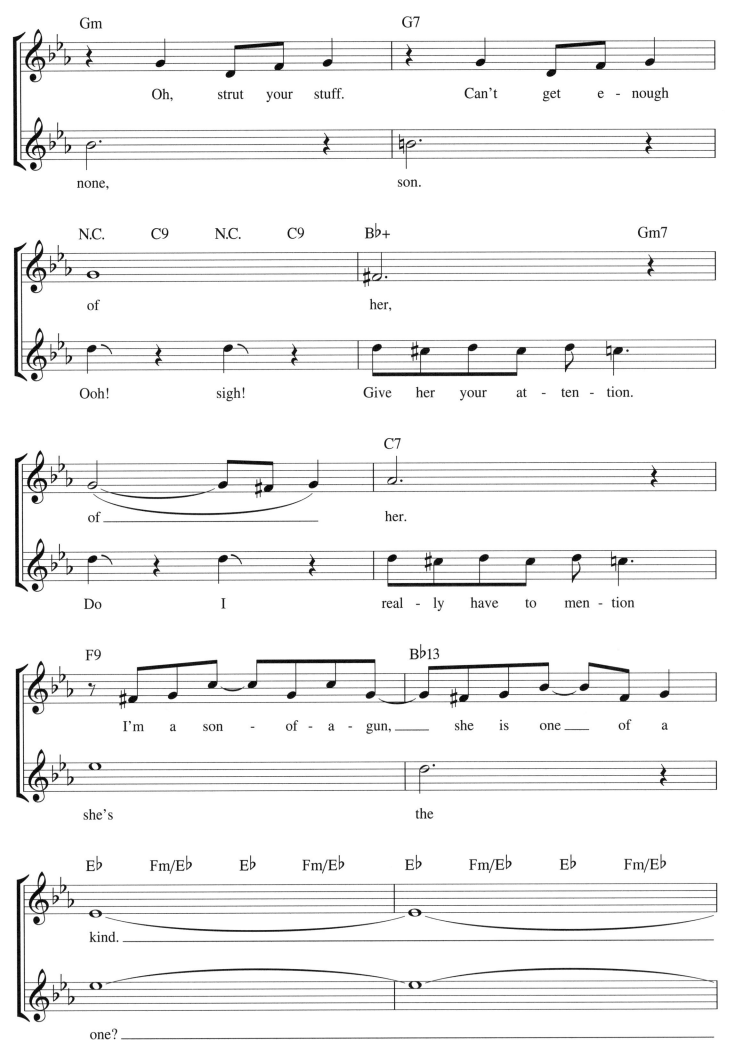

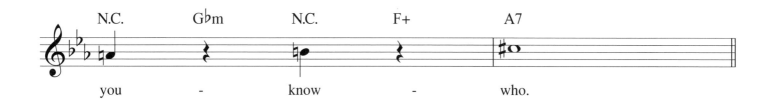

you - know - who.

Chorus

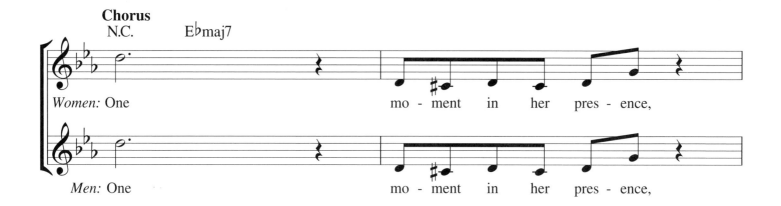

Women: One mo - ment in her pres - ence,

Men: One mo - ment in her pres - ence,

and you can for - get the rest,

and you can for - get the rest,

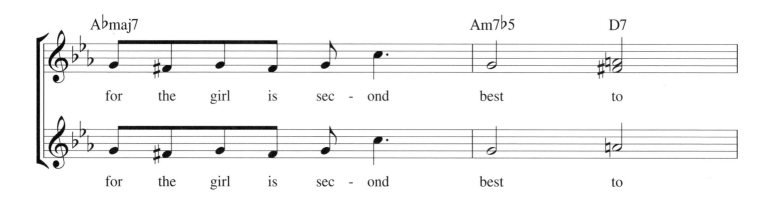

for the girl is sec - ond best to

for the girl is sec - ond best to

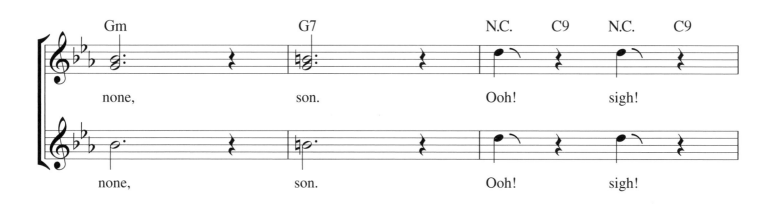

none, son. Ooh! sigh!

none, son. Ooh! sigh!

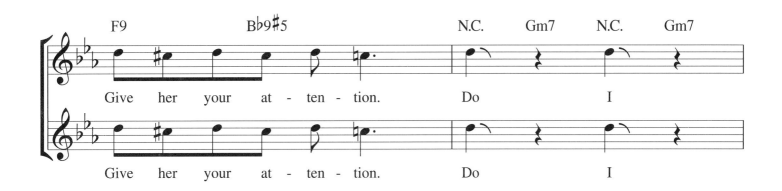

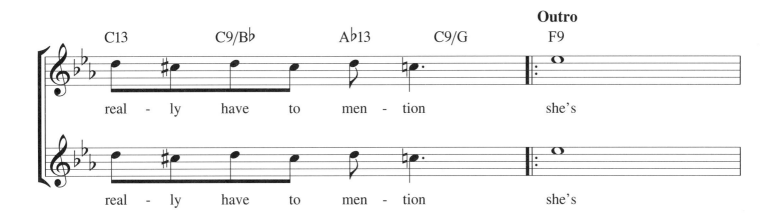

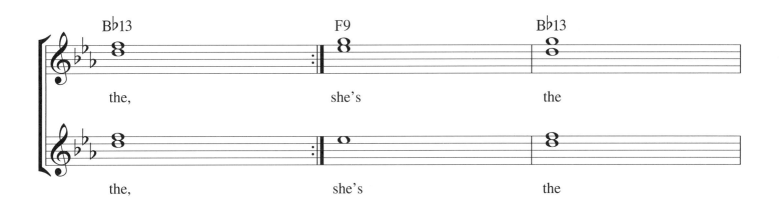

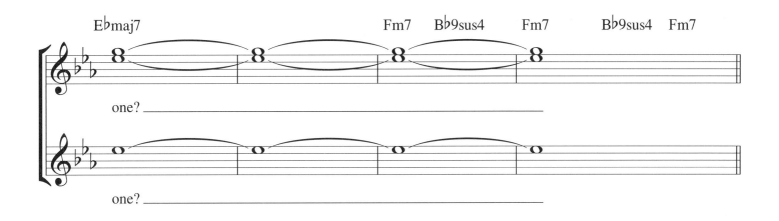

People

from FUNNY GIRL
Words by Bob Merrill
Music by Jule Styne

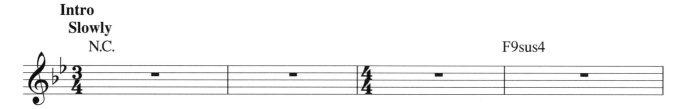

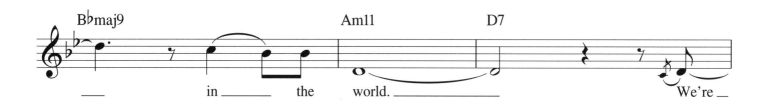

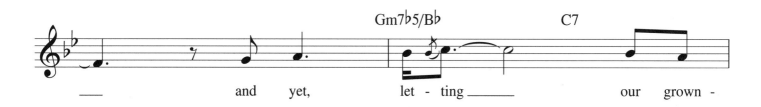

She (He) Touched Me

from DRAT! THE CAT!

Lyric by Ira Levin
Music by Milton Schafer

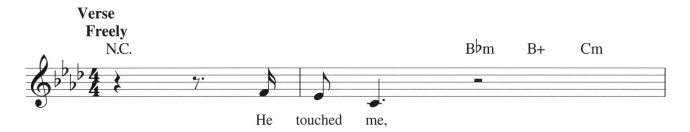

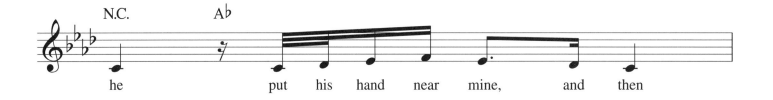

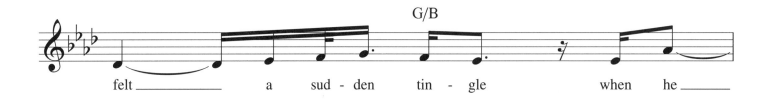

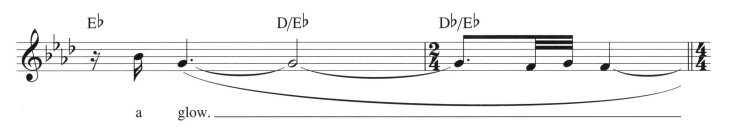

He knew it, _____

it _____ was-n't _____ ac - ci - den - tal. _____ No, _____

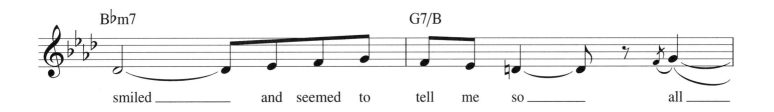

_____ he knew it. _____ He

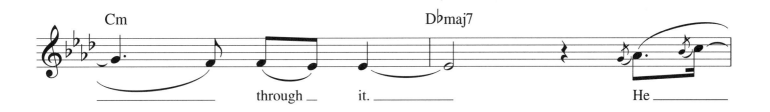

smiled _____ and seemed to tell me so _____ all _____

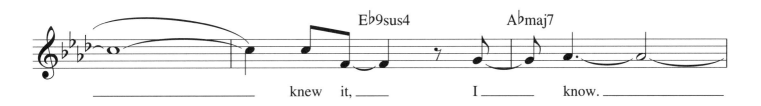

_____ through _ it. _____ He _____

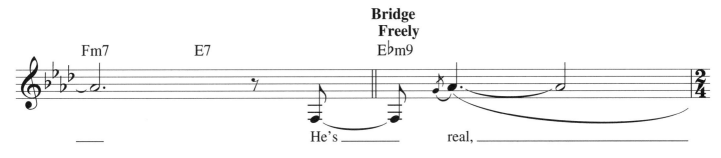

_____ knew it, _____ I _____ know. _____

Bridge
Freely

_____ He's _____ real, _____

the world is a-live _____ and shin - ing. _____

I feel _____ such a

won - der - ful drive _____ toward _ val - en -

Verse
Moderately

tin - ing. He touched me. _____

_____ I sim - ply have to face _ the fact.

He touched me. _____ Con -

trol my - self _ and try to act as if I re -

mem - ber _____ my _____ name, _____

Tomorrow

from the Musical Production ANNIE

Lyric by Martin Charnin
Music by Charles Strouse

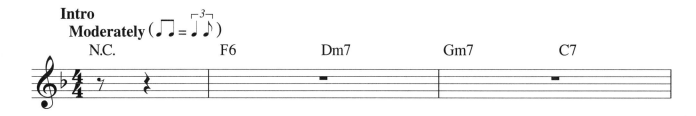

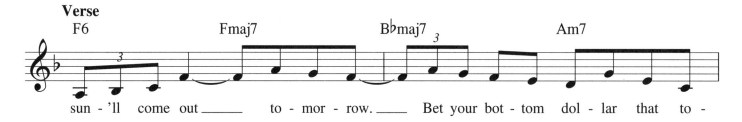

The

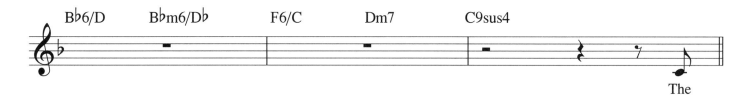

sun - 'll come out ___ to - mor - row. ___ Bet your bot - tom dol - lar that to -

mor - row there'll be ___ sun. ___ Just

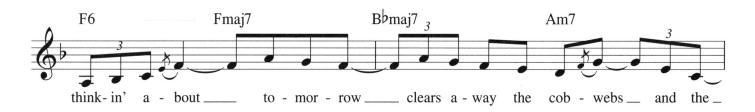

think - in' a - bout ___ to - mor - row ___ clears a - way the cob - webs ___ and the ___

Interlude

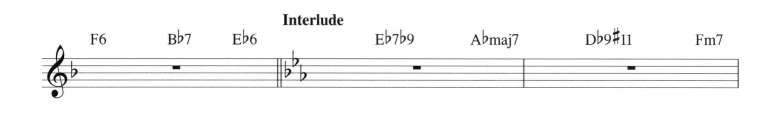

The

Verse

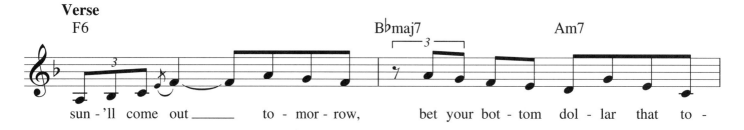

sun - 'll come out _____ to - mor - row, bet your bot - tom dol - lar that to -

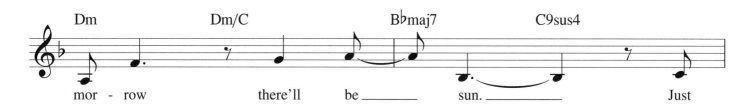

mor - row there'll be _____ sun. _____ Just

think - in' a - bout _____ to - mor - row _____ clears a - way the cob - webs _ and the

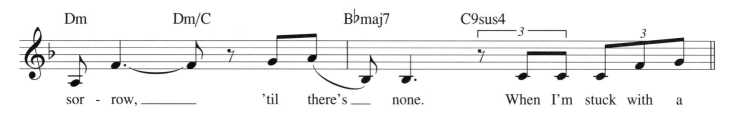

sor - row, _____ 'til there's _ none. When I'm stuck with a

Bridge

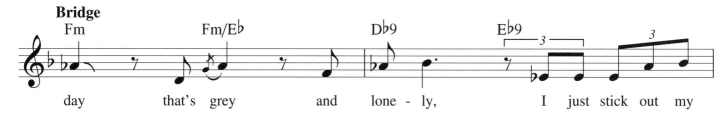

day that's grey and lone - ly, I just stick out my

chin and grin and _____ say, _____

Unusual Way
(In a Very Unusual Way)

from NINE

Words and Music by Maury Yeston

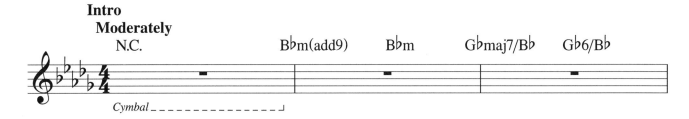

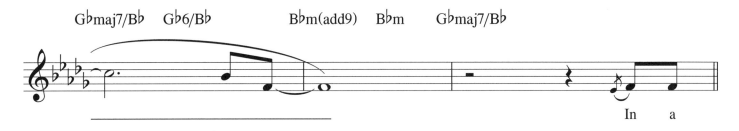

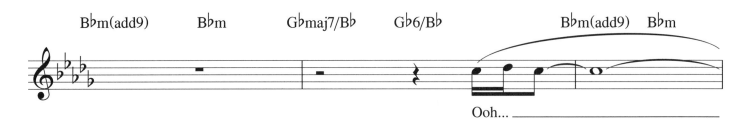

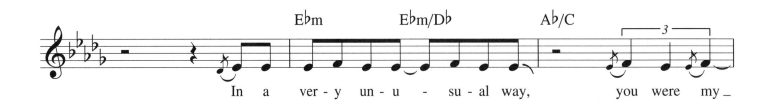

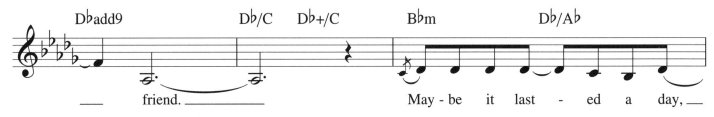

why,   you're the rea - son   why. _____

Bridge

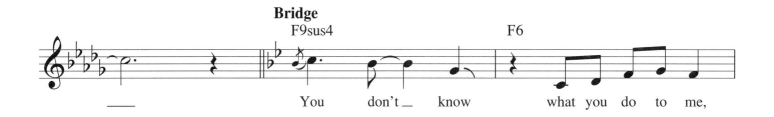

_____   You don't _ know   what you do to me,

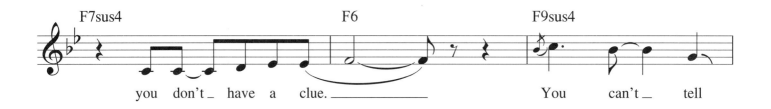

you don't _ have a clue. _____   You can't _ tell

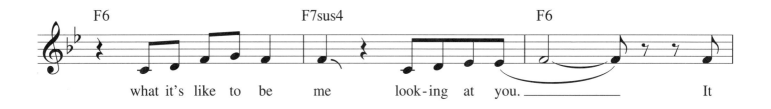

what it's like to be me   look-ing at you. _____   It

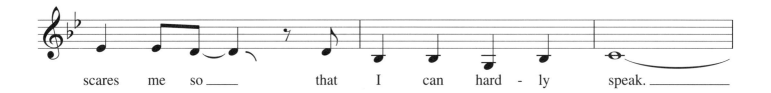

scares me so ____ that I can hard - ly speak. _____

Verse

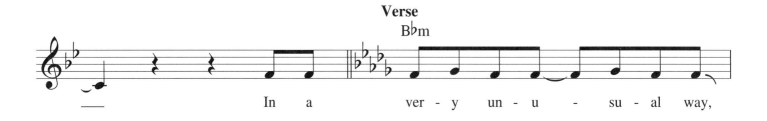

_____   In a ver - y un - u - su - al way,

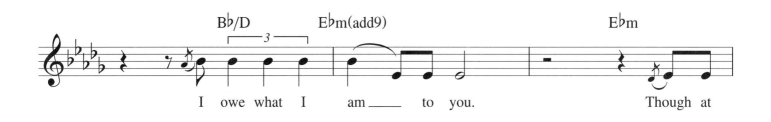

I owe what I am ____ to you.   Though at

times it ap - pears ___ I won't stay, I nev - er ___ go. ___

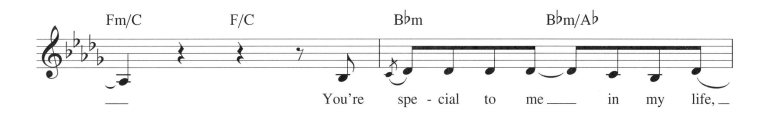

___ You're spe - cial to me ___ in my life, ___

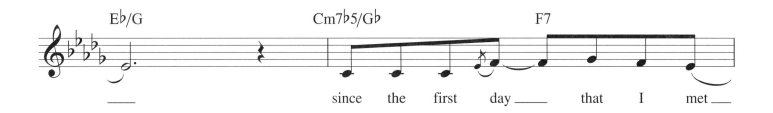

___ since the first day ___ that I met ___

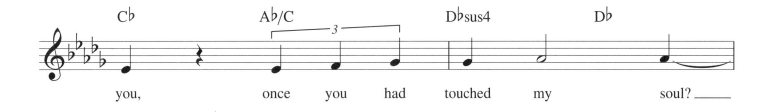

___ you. ___ How could I ev - er for - get

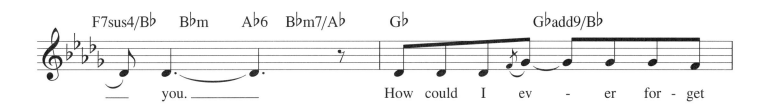

you, once you had touched my soul? ___

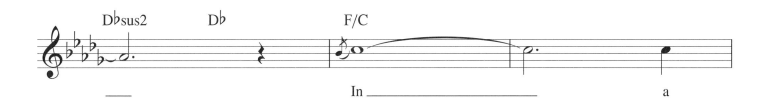

In ___ a

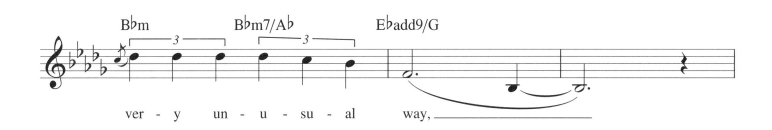

ver - y un - u - su - al way, ___

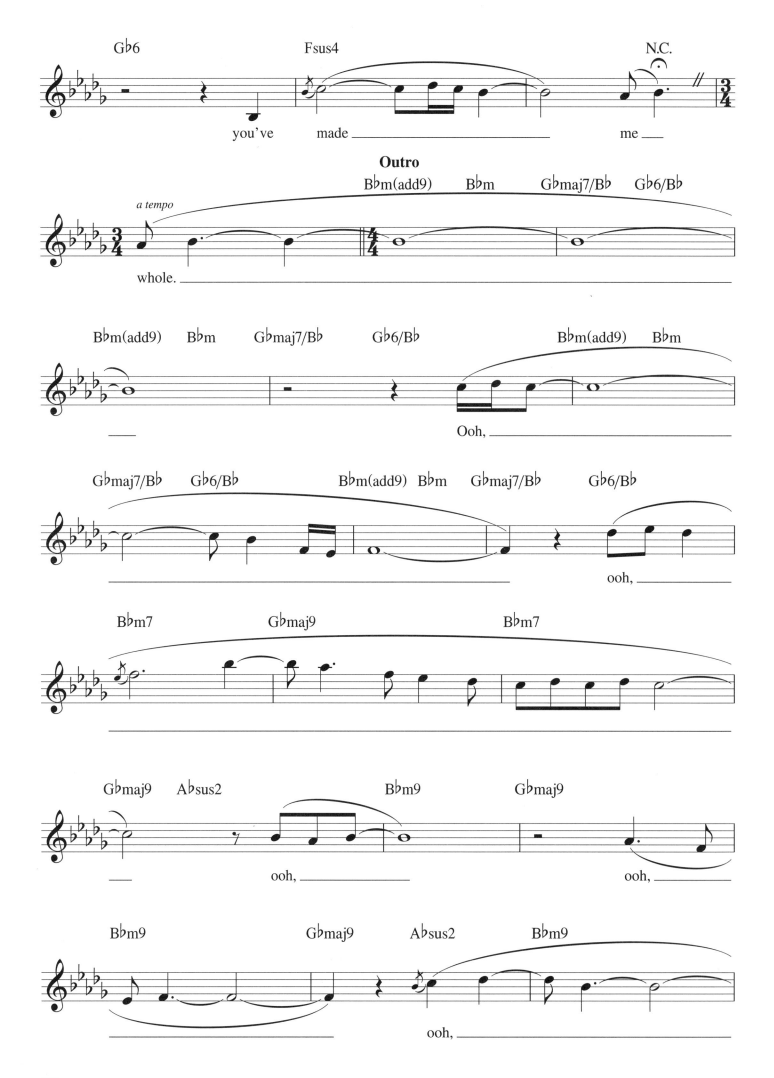

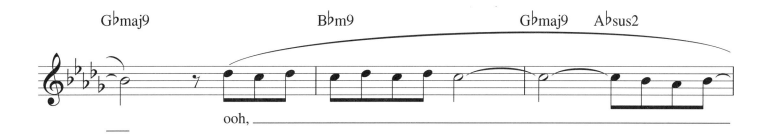

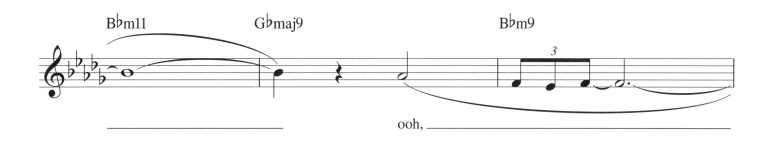

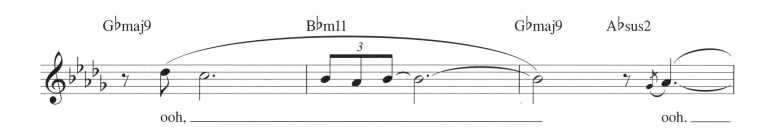

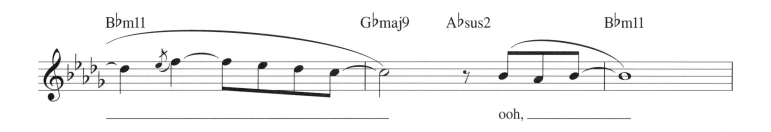

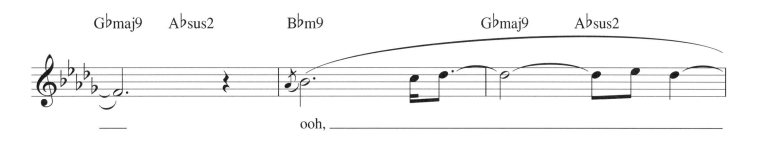

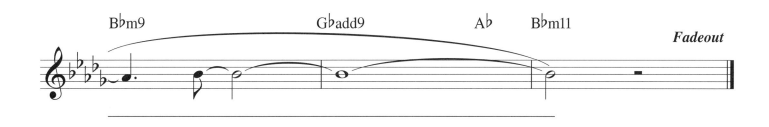

What I Did for Love

from A CHORUS LINE

Music by Marvin Hamlisch
Lyric by Edward Kleban

love's what we'll re - mem - ber.

Verse

Kiss to - day good - bye,

and point me toward to - mor - row.

We did what we had to do.

Won't for - get can't re - gret what I

did for love, what I did for

love, what I did for

Outro
Slowly

love.